SUPER-LIVING

PSYCHOLOGICAL SURVIVAL 101 MANUAL FOR LOCKDOWNS AND FOR THE NEW WORLD 🇬🇧

"Based on the bilingual psychological manual *Super-viv(i)ente*
published in Italy, Spain and UK as New Voice for Postcovid World"

Luca Povoleri (De Las Heras)

English empowered by: Shenda Cregan

New Voices

Essay Collection

Translated from the original book
"Super-viv(i)ente" by Luca Povoleri De Las Heras
Published in Europe on October 2020
by Gruppo Albatros Il Filo

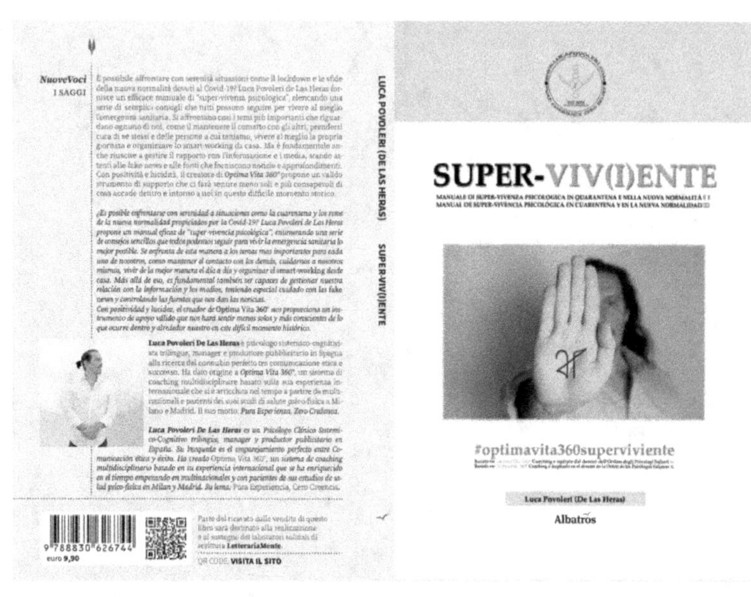

Original book: "Super-viv(i)ente" by Luca Povoleri De Las Heras,, Italian and Spanish version.

© 2020 Gruppo Albatros Il Filo S.r.L. Roma

www.gruppoalbatros.com – info@gruppoalbatros.com

ISBN 9788830626744

1ª edizione Ottobre 2020

Luca Povoleri De Las Heras

Super-Living

PSYCHOLOGICAL SURVIVAL 101 MANUAL FOR LOCKDOWNS AND FOR THE NEW WORLD

"Based on the bilingual psychological manual *Super-viv(i)ente*, published in Italy, Spain and UK as New Voice for Postcovid World"

A world of gratitude to my husband Peter
for supporting every part of the project
and for lending me his photographic creativity
to create immediacy and a natural focus.

A word of gratitude to Shenda
english-spanish Life Adventurer
of Design and Furniture Creation
that empowered my english translation
with the same talent, boldness and passion
you can find in her outstanding art creations.

Collaborators:

Photo: Peter López de Las Heras
English Proofreading: Shenda Cregan

New Voices Collection
Introduction by Barbara Alberti

Professor. Robin Ian Dunbar, an English anthropologist, took time out to study for how many friends human beings can really count on. The final result was very limited, but the Professor forgot about the books, which are limited only by the human lifespan.

It's the one real lover, the book. A true confidant that doesn't betray you and never abandons you. A personal friend of mine, a tireless reader, said to me once: *I'll have as many lives as I can read about. I will be all the characters I wish to be...*

A book gives you two different gifts fused together: you can find yourself in it and you can find a truce with your identity. Better than anyone, Emily Dickinson said in one of her most famous verses:

There is no Frigate like a Book
To take us Lands away
Nor any Coursers like a Page
Of prancing Poetry –
This Traverse may the poorest take
Without oppress of Toll –

How frugal is the Chariot
That bears the Human Soul –

Sometimes, as a victim of unshareable feelings you think you're insane, you find your visions guilty and futile, unworthy to rise to the dignity of *facts* and you don't dare to confess them to anyone, as they feel so absurd to you.

But one day you will find them in a novel. Someone else confessed the same visions, maybe a long time ago. Alone, only you in front of the page, you have the right to be absolute. The book is the most gentle picklock to hack into reality. It is the translation of a dream.

In my past, as teenagers, we were forced to hide when reading a book, as most of the books in the house were forbidden to young people. Shakespear, even Fogazzaro was suspicious, reading Ovidio was sure reason for corporal punishment.
Collodi was permitted, the Struwwelpeter, the canine London and the lives of the saints.

On Christmas Eve my cousin was found in the attic reading the most forbidden book among the forbidden books, *Lady Chatterley's Lover*. He was punished by being left out of the Christmas celebrations, no gifts and banned from Christmas dinner with ignominy. I found him later in the corridor totaly unmortified by it at all, instead he was mildly swaggering, he seemed even taller than usual. He opened his jacket, and revealed he was carrying the 4 volumes of *Peace and War* and he said to me: "Who cares for Christmas dinner. This year I'll celebrate Christmas at Rostov's.".

They are patient, the books, they wait for us standing there, showing their backs on the shelves all life long, and they are able to wait forever for you to open them.

Everyone love their favorite writers as if they were part of their own family, but we also love some translators or prefaces authors, the ones that initiate us into the mystery of another language, of another world.

Some voices define us as much as the one we use every day, sometimes even more so, but they're never enough. So when more of them turn up, they can be an incredible gift, one that you can't bare to part with.

This is the spirit of Albatros, while offering us it's **New Voices** collection, a selection of new italian authors, references for the sailing reader, like having one arm bound tight to the main mast to avoid the call of the beckoning sirens, the other above your eyes to enjoy the vastity of the horizon. The publisher, who makes the journey real, is now giving you the most awarded italian publishing collection of emerging authors. If you are not a believer in awards you can believe in the readers thanks for whom this is one of the most best-selling collections.

In the sea of those words written waiting to be read, we'll find ourselves again with new memories, new paths. *New voices, New rooms.*

How to read Super-living

"Super-viv(i)ente" was a book on a pandemic psychological survival manual, containing around 16% of the therapeutic principles of "Optima Vita 360*". Some people may think that's too little, but the purpose is to write a book that people can read without training. It's in your eyes the chance to read between lines and know the author to reach deeper meanings.

You will find some inspiration here and some shards of truth, you can use them while learning how to be a better narrator of your life. As Life Adventurers in training you're going to learn about co-creation and self-narration. Use them wisely...

"Super-living" is a non-literal translation of "Super-viv(i)ente" made after a year of Covid-19 pandemic. Some implicits may have changed from the original book to adapt to the new reality, but the spirit is the same.

And this is the way you should read it and use it, in orderd to fully exploit it's empowering and shielding effects.

1. Read the book entirely. It's a 3h reading book.

2. Don't hurry to finish. Enjoy. There are strong implicits to explore in every sentence.

3. After you read it, use it like an I Ching book: when you feel you need a power up or a relaxing time, open it and read a line.

Remember that "Optima Vita 360*" philosophy is universal, so if you're reading this after Covid 19 pandemic, try to apply it to your daily life.

It's a good exercise for every aspect of your existence to be able to find the essence inside everything, to go behind the walls and the masks of reality to find that seed of truth that we're losing in the post-truth world.

This book is attempting to summon a new world and you can be part of it by living your life to the fullest, focusing on your narrative while always remembering you're part of something bigger.

Author's Note

"Super-viv(i)ente" was published in Europe in october 2020 as a bilingual manual in Spanish and Italian by one of the most important publishers for emerging authors as "New Voices" for the (Post)Covid world.

This manual, which is already available in the best bookstores of Italy, Spain and the UK, is a "Psychological First Aid Guide" for the Covid-19 pandemic and for the transition into the new normality for all English-speaking people, but also a very practical guide to super-live everyday life.

"Super" here is not about "superheroes" like a cheap coaching slogan, it is used as in the original latin meaning "above" and it's definition will be clear at the end of your reading. Every human is able to super-live in my experience, as super-living psychology is universal, so you have a choice in front of you. Maybe at the end of this manual you can see it as the most viable one and join the universal and equal human being movement toward the future.

This is my voice, supported by a very strong publisher that I want to thank for believing in my message and it's been empowered by the thorough work of another Life Adventurer I'm honored to call my friend: Shenda Cregan, a bilingual English-Spanish and amazingly creative designer that lended her homeland language skills to proofread the "Super-viv(i)ente" international project.

In English "Super-viv(i)ente" literally means "Super-living person", so we translated it as "Super-living". The original title was a game of words between italian and spanish with just that "(i)" separating two cultures, two entire worlds of people of the same human species having everything in common.

Language can't be a barrier forever so this project is to open a door, to create a bridge, between "Super-living" human beings. Together. Stronger.

This humble and compact book is the translation of the original bilingual one, with all the small linguistic imperfection of an author who loves all the 3 languages he speaks. It was born during the first 2020 covid lockdown, a moment that brought a lot of people to worry about the present but also to look at a #postcovid19 future.

The ideas represented here are useful during lockdown and quarantine, but also in all the following stages to adapt and create the new normality.

The project is a personal revision of some of the indications of the "Ordine degli Psicologi Italiani" (the

Official Italian Psychologists Association) written by an italian-spanish psychologist whose objective is to empower the human and practical side of their message through my "Optima Vita 360°" Psychological Coaching System.

My intention is to send this message in the widest possible way with simple and accessible words. I hope I can do that thanks to my husband's collaboration for the creative and visual part as well as the photos that open every chapter.

In my opinion this is a really necessary action to counteract the effects of collective fear, sensationalism, counterinformation and fake news that many times have circulated wildly while poisoning our communication with family and friends.

Our common objective is to fight with all our strength this frustration, the apparent helplessness generating anxiety, terror and sometimes at the contrary the illusion of immunity, born from a situation that is affecting the entire world. Trying to look for "information" in places where we know that they are manipulated like social network, apparently "free" video platforms, apps, news channels etc... is the worst idea and sometimes the only option we feel we have. But if we add this need to "information" together with the aforementioned fear and frustration, it creates a nefarious triumvirate that enforces the culture of psychological terrorism associated to Coronavirus Psychologica and Social Construct and becomes a very powerful common enemy. One that just a few are aware of.

Covid Construct is maybe an enemy worse than the virus itself because it reaches everyone, at every distance, at every time. Economy, society, work, relationships... everything is infected and the real problem is that even when the sanitary emergency will be over, some people will be completely and utterly still a victim of this Construct.

That's why this book is meant to be a psychological first aid kit for your mind, hopefully maybe even a good vaccine.

Fear will make our social and economical recuperation far slower than the medical one and everyone that are immune or protected by this can help accelerate the new world to manifest.

Try to get information only from official sources and public health communication channels. Every other idea, including this book, just consider it as "inspiration" and incentive to be aware of yourself and of the world around you.

Even if our evolution made us pass through a phase of exasperated individualism, the philosophy that underlies and nurtures this project considers the human being as a "citizen", meaning someone who can keep his individuality and still think about collectivity. Extremisms have been the worst of the plagues throughout our history and this common enemy can offer the perfect occasion to learn moderation and put aside the reactive quick response that keeps excluded part of the population for the benefit of a few.

Public health as much as scientific research is the only defense we have. We need to value them in the present and in the future as the main sources of knowledge and care of the human being.

Civic awareness then, in my opinion, taken as a value that is of the person as an individual and the people as community at the same time, has to be the final solution when facing the decision of our governments. The pride we can feel in seeing citizens like myself and like you that try to follow the instructions while being aware of their meaning and not only for legal imposition has to be our guide. Citizens of the community. That is the feeling that has to fill our heart and minds of the right kind of motivation to adapt and evolve as persons and society.

The world was moving much faster than usual in the last few years, that's true and we may have to slow down a little in the future, but maybe it's not necessary to slow down too much. Instead we can keep a steady step (and a sustainable one too) adding maybe just a little more of collective introspection with a little more of generosity toward our fellow humans.

For this reason let's take care for ourselves in these quarantine times and in this new world, but at the same time let's build up our attention to what's going to happen after the pandemic. This way the #postcovi19 will be as important as our actual present and it may be more oriented to finding the essence of things and to select those people who inspire us and those who can stay near us.

Let's begin to consider the human being not for it's difference (which is nourishment for extremisms), but for the value for a common destiny actively shared with each other.

With Strength, Love and Positive Energy.
LPdLH

#optimavita360superviviente

1) *Manage stress and develop resilience*

Resilience = Resistance + Flexibility + Ability to adapt.

It's not only a matter of resistance, we're talking about transforming yourself along with the situation without losing yourself in the process. That goes by the idea that you won't lose yourself if you change part of you in order to live a better everyday life. Try to use this time to check your habits and use the situation to improve them or to change them.

These worldwide events don't happen to you as the absolute main character of a tv show. During Covid-19 pandemic we find ourselves in a common challenge so we may feel bad about it, but even in normal times self-pity (or "self-compassion") is the strongest temptation and still the worst solution. Beyond the fact that this movement of the soul makes you less effective in awakening your hidden resources (and you have them), seeing yourself as the victim in front of the challenge is like a baby cry, it's a very powerful help request, one that is hard to ignore. This time though it's a request for an exaggerated level of attention you don't really need. The danger is to hurt your loved ones...

"False positives" in scientific research are events that appears to be the one you're expecting, but in the end they're not.
The same thing is the "Serial Victimist" main cours of action. Clearly we're not talking of serial killer victims but of those normal people that are always desperate and unseemingly victims of the worst series of unlucky or hostile events and situations. So much it almost "feels" (and we can all feel it) like it's a way of life, not a real thing. Self-pity (or "self-compassion") is a "low

cost" option of our cognitive system, so sometimes we prefer this instead of getting our act together and this creates a culture were co-dependency becomes a game of victims and saviours (or heroes). Let's try to leave this to the past... we have to accept who we are, but at the same time we can try to be our best version of ourselves.

Let's try to see stress, sadness, anxiety and very emotion produced by quarantine, or by staying at home, or by living stuck in our city and in a world with reduced vital and work needs, like a challenge for your mind skills. Let your imagination go free, read something, connect with friends, follow some video influencer that makes you feel better or entertained. And take the time to analize all this connection and see if some of them has to be resized.

There's no need to be perfect, fit or "performative" here, we have to stay home the days we need to stay home, thinking that there will be an end to this. You have to be strong for the world that is coming next. That world will be a challenge... staying at home will seem nothing in comparison. In fact while vaccinating we're already seeing a glimpse of the problems we're going to be facing very soon.

So try to be easygoing and use a soothing attitude when you're talking to others. No one wants to feel bad because of you and it's true that you can and "have to" find a way to communicate your negative emotions (Check point 5), but remember that everyone in the right conditions has a warrior's soul.

At the same time and just as opposites of "Serial Victims" try not to be a "Imperturbable Hero". It is important and human to feel sadness and desperation. Don't reject them.

Crying can be healthy if it's a way to express an emotion, but only if it's not the only way to express it. On the contrary, if you think that being impervious to your emotions is the best way to face this moment, follow your instincts, but remember that every human has a vast interior world and what you block from reaching to your rational mind will be felt by your body anyway.

Stress can hide unexpected gifts if we accept it as a personal challenge. We can increase our motivation to face stress with all the tools we can imagine. Try to see yourself as a person with the active power to change the situation. Let's use some (self)irony and humour too, not only to flee from reality for a moment (what would be the price for that if you'd do it all the time?), but also to make our efforts easier.

Everyone of you can do his/her part and we can

all be useful. Try to carry your own weight the best you can, being sure you're really doing it the best you can and not only "saying it". If you are able to ask for help, even by reluctantly swallowing your pride or to stop asking for help for everything, accepting your inner strength, you'll find out that people you care about are going to be there for you even without asking.

And after this emergency everything you transformed yourselves into will give you even greater satisfaction. Try and see for yourself...

2) Awaken your dormant gifts

Many people will say that this pandemic is a war where we're all united against an "enemy of mankind". Even if the military comparison may be a little excessive to some sensibilities, the truth behind this idea is that only together we can co-create the solution.

Another aspect of our experience that we can

optimize is to use the stress of these moments to "hack" our genetics waking up dormant resources we don't even know about.

Stress is a disease because it represents a continuous and prolonged reaction to persisting stimuli of any origin (meaning events, emotions, facts) during the day. Even when they do not exist. Usually it would be naturally associated with high performance situations or highly riskful activities, but in reality it presents itself in the same way even in averagely and low performance/low risk situations of everyday life. That's because we instinctively decide inside of us what we "feel" like performative or riskful for our identity or psycho-physical integrity (meaning body, mind and emotions) and we apply it to situations that have no such objective value. So we live stress, sometimes even when it's not really there.

Being the cause of this stress real or just "felt like real", the best way you can defend yourself in a practical way, is trying to reduce our psychological and physical "activation". Meaning when you feel stress, find a way to relax the body, trying not to anaesthetize yourselves in the process (so chemistry is not the best way).

In some circumstances the collective stress may awaken those dormant gifts that during an averagely stressed life (there is no such thing as a "relaxed life" without anaesthetizing it) are destined to stay in the shadows of our genetics. If you're feeling stressed out, try using the same strategies and actions you take to cope with it normally, but try this: in "Optima Vita 360°" we try to be one with our stress. So ask yourself what the stress can teach you to awaken your talents, instead of focusing on reducing the damage. These talents are much needed for you to Super-live life (Check point 12).

The Official Italian Psychologists Association suggests learning to get bored. We live overcharged with stimuli from outside ourselves and this can bring °us too far from that sometimes-useful silence we need to hear our inner voice. Maybe it's not Beyoncé's voice, but in our secret garden there are treasures we didn't even begin to look for only because we live all our lives looking at someone else's public gardens.

3) Celebrate every moment of the day

The ritualism, the symbolism and the magic of taking your coffee in the morning, to perfectly wipe the edges of the sink in the kitchen, to open the windows to let fresh air get in. Try to think of all the movements you're doing to execute those simple actions day after day. Hundreds of muscles and thousands of biolectrical discharges flow through your body only to turn on the light in the bathroom. You are a living storm!

When you feel sad, bored or tormented by the quarantine or by the problems of an uncertain future try to empower every action doing it slower, like in a "slow motion" scene. Begin from the easy ones like taking a pen or writing a message and you'll already see a probably interesting change of perspective. You have not to stay in a slow motion mode, we're talking about isolated actions. In fact the more isolated, the better, especially at the beginning.

When quarantines and restrictions will be over, you may have not had that many occasions to experiment and enjoy this voluntary slowdown of your life rhythms, but for a while you may keep the feeling and the augmented awareness that you obtained by celebrating every aspect of the day. Maybe at that moment, one we're so eager to see, when new normality will be here, you can try to use this exercise to better deal with any new challenging situations.

Besides you will have the advantage to realize the quantity of energy you actually use for your activities and that will help you to deal with the stress eating or the emotional hunger that may catch you when you're feeling bored or anxious.

Another way to celebrate your day is to find a

new alimentary balance. Take your time to check your diet. Do not blame yourself too much if the feeling of imprisonment is compromising the steadiness you had before, but try not to "eat your emotions" or to starve them by taking a strict diet you will surely revert in the future. Find moderation and reject extreme changes even if you may consider a lowered intake of calories if you're moving less.

If you think you need sugar, try to think about what you're feeling at that moment and, if you decide to have one of those "snacks" that can provide light to an entire city for an hour do it, but with heart!
Eat it slowly, enjoy every bite with all the pleasure you deserve to try.

Self-blaming for your physical state or for losing your fit state is already a very poor response in normal situations to motivate you to a healthy diet, but in quarantine it's the worst thing you can do to yourself. If you reduce your food extremely you're just killing your emotions as much as if you're overeating, do not think that cheap social confirmation will shield you from emotional distress.

If you overindulge yourself, do it breathing deeply a couple times before and using your 5 senses. Smelling the food is an essential part of taste and we lose it almost everyday for acquired automatism, lack of knowledge or an altered sense of self-awareness that makes you feel ridiculous to smell your food while eating it because of social pressure. Take a close look at your food and concentrate on the visual change of your dish while you're eating it. Focus on the movements of your hand, your face and your mouth while chewing your food and try to recognize and separate every shade of taste by self-checking the differences between the first and the following bites. Last but not least, don't forget to feel your environment through the noises, the words and the music around you.

For your diet, as much as for other aspects of life, find a way to create a dedicated time to the activity you're doing trying to avoid "multitasking". And if you can give priority to fruit, vegetables, meat and fish as main dishes, trying to keep a balanced diet with good fat and carbs... well that would be even better.

4) *Manage your negative emotions*

Fear, sadness, anger and frustration. We're stuck at home or at least very limited in our movements, unable to travel, the world stopped for months, then went back moving at a slower pace and it's very different from before. Don't even start to think of those who don't follow the health authorities and destroy social distancing collective effort by acting for themselves. Those false rebels who seem unaffected by the situation (but is that true?) and do whatever they want without thinking about the consequences they have on the common fight may undermine your security and willpower.

There are many reasons that can create negativity and it's important to deal with them when they appear to avoid them creating a critical mass and discharge their chaotic effects on your life.

Here the key is using the power of self-awareness: "I feel angered", "I feel sad"... It is important to "feel" and not "be" while dealing with this emotions. When you "feel" something, somehow you're saying to your mind that you "are not" that feeling and that you can live it without it threatening your emotional world.

"I'm angry...", "I'm sad..." on the contrary, which means "being" that emotion, sends a message to your mind that all your inner world is overlapping with that emotion. It's unrealistic and false, avoid it, there's more of you in you.

Another aspect and maybe a deeper one, is that there may not be such things as "negative" emotions as lot's of people say.

In "Optima Vita 360°" I always suggest trying to consider those supposedly negative emotions like "different allies" because they still send very important information to super-live your day, and there's more to it... Do not anesthetize them, instead relax your body by breathing to get in a deeper and more honest contact with yourself.

There's no need to use exotic named oriental breathing techniques to do that... try to listen to your "natural rhythm" which means "focus your attention on when your lungs tell you to inflate and deflate them, trying as much as you can to not interfere". Your best effort is the best effort you need.

Now that you're centered as much as you can (you won't be seeing magic bells, mystical lights or strange sensations... just breathe...) then ask yourself "What does this sadness/anger/frustration... want to tell me?"

Try not to think of the big picture now, focus on your daily reality and try to reach a mediation with those feelings. Maybe they're not nice ones, but they are real enough. You can consider them like people you don't like and still have to or even want to live with you. They're neighbours that you may have problems with but that share part of your garden and you don't want too many problems, do you? Yes, here you can use your creativity and talk to yourself as if you were talking to a friend and say "If I were you...". Every idea is a good idea!

Last piece of mind: try to ask these emotions to find satisfaction in something you have control over. For instance, let's take those "different allies" created by huge topics like "The situation of your Country", "The public figure Mister-so-and-so that said that thing", "Covid-19 pandemic" which are things you have from limited to almost no direct control over.

Now try to see the first one "The situation of your Country", as the situation of your house and let's use the suggestions of your "different ally" (the emotions that surges from that concept) to motivate you to try and think of different way to change your similar problems in your house as if it was the "big picture" itself. There are always analogies you can use.

If your emotions are aroused for the "The public figure Mister-so-and-so that said that thing" instead, don't vent it online to nourish this emotion with the feedback of people thinking the same as you (that's worse than high-calorie snacks for you Ego).
Try instead to own this anger by looking in your daily life when you act in a similar way (everyone acts in ways that can be improved), find the inspiration in your apparent enemy and find a way to avoid that behaviour when you see it in yourself.

If it's the "Covid-19 pandemic" the problem for

you (and for everyone), finding a "different ally" in this is quite simple: keep a healthy life physically, emotionally and in your relationship with others. That will keep your immune defenses high and on this you have enough control to make it a good active goal.

In wider terms, try to produce good emotions for you and share it with your friends and family. This way you'll be stronger and with everyone who deserves it.

5) *Share your feelings... but remember to listen!*

We are used to sharing coffee in the morning, hot selfies and funny memes... why can't we try and share our worries too? This helps to process them.

Furthermore, verbally communicating your mood and worries helps to balance their emotional charge. Always remember point 1 though... let's try avoiding "Serial Victimism" while doing that.

If you share your feelings or your ideas on a matter, always offer to listen to the other ones too. Then you can respect their freedom to do it or not to. Remember that we're on the same boat and everyone can find relief in someone available to listen to them. Although of course it's not your profession, so remember that to yourself and to the others, to avoid burn up.

Sometimes we feel that sharing is a form of weakness and that listening is a form of strength, but this time let's just focus on the attention we give and receive with these two actions. Yes, sharing can be a strength, oversharing instead can be a weakness.

Listening can be strength (and power, remember this when someone doesn't share as much as you do). At the same time it can be a form of weakness too for those who only listen to others for fear of their own thoughts and emotions.

This means that whether you share or listen, always do it with the intention to reciprocate: that may be the best way to take and to give the best part of both interactions.

In a relational fair-trade, which should be the same as any transaction between two entities but with emotional resources instead of money, there is always an element of helpfulness in both parts through your strengths, your experiences or even just through your emotional availability.

Just remember that if you feel this kind of helping relationship is too much for you, that means that you could rely on professional aid for you or as a suggestion to the other. That works during the pandemic and after that.

Now, as we clarified our baseline on communication let's see in detail how we have to adapt it depending on the different vital phases of the person we're communicating with.

a) Listen to children!

In our history we went completely off-board when we tried to treat our children like little adults. That was because children were a labour force, so the earlier they were seen as adults, the earlier they would work for free...

In fact when you see children who seem more mature than their age, it is very likely it is not a good thing even if it seems funny. Excessively adult-minded children may be that way because their environment (meaning everything they receive by their role models in family, school, networks etc...) are much more stressful than they should experience at their age. We have to protect them from ourselves sometimes because even love can be an occasion to lose perspective on the differences between children mind and ours. At the same time we shouldn't make the mistake of thinking that children are made of glass.

Try to speak to your child about the situation without lying to her/him. If you like, maybe you can use a game to talk to him/her. Lies sometimes can be scarier and more confusing for them than a truth, even a difficult one to accept. Children can unconsciously understand there's false information out there in your communication. They don't have a fully shaped mind or a cognitive independence to understand what is wrong with it, but they experience the stress produced by the contrast between a lie from a caregiver (someone they actually love and depend on) and the same caregivers emotions that reveal the lie. Children can instinctively read your feelings.

Truth can be shared by a game, a song, images, stories, everything that can be appropriate to their age group. Try to use the same vocabulary they use, their words. It's important to hear them out and give them the chance to express their feelings through a hobby or any kind of creative effort during their free time.

At the same time it is important to keep their

education up to speed with the indication of the school.

Even if the world has slowed down at the moment, they will not stop growing.

b) Listen to teenagers!

If you think it's hard for an adult to stay home and not meet their friends and loved ones, many teenagers are just creating their social (and Social... different but both valid) networks and this situation it can be extremely hard for them. After the lockdowns they may be able to meet with their friends, but with many restrictions and with a very dense experience on their shoulders.

Try to pay attention to their subtexts, what they really want to say. It may be a good moment to talk to them and accept their vocabulary sometimes far from our own (you don't really need to use it too though... understanding and accepting it is enough).

You may judge or underestimate their sometimes original or exotic way of expressing themselves, but those words hide the thoughts of a mind very very near to the adult one, so they deserve attention.

They have to keep up the pace with their education too as indicated by the educational institutions they're attending and it could be a good time to share some responsibilities at home.

This is not only about doing chores, it is a time to listen to their ideas on your family and to share their feelings about it. It can be an occasion to find that you share the same feelings on some important family topics. Or not.

Let them keep their connections with friends and create a shared family schedule giving value to their personal talents. Give them the responsibility that you may be reluctant to give them when you have less time to spend with them and let yourself be surprised by what they can actually do, ready to support them in their growth, but without focusing too much on them achieving the goal.

Focus your attention (and theirs) on the processes they use to do that. Remember to give them realistic objectives for their age too: very frequently our society gives them goals so hard that are almost unachievable. A teenager with a generally good self-esteem is better than a frustrated achiever, although, as always, reality resides somewhere in the middle. In fact, try not to have excessively low expectations neither: it is important to give them some challenges that help them to grow up.

We're talking about persons that can feel a higher need of seeing their friends than the adults so give them the space for their hobbies, for videogames with some form of social interaction and for their Social Network time, *"Cum Grano Salis"* (latin say meaning "with a grain of salt", meaning "with moderation") as always. In these historical moments it may be better to give some more freedom than the usual, creating a sharing and accepting space inside the four walls of your house instead of exploiting your supremacy to control your domestic territory. Of course your house is not a jungle neither, freedom means always referring to an accomodating environment in respect of the freedom of the others inside.

During emotionally intense moments, try to avoid escalation and acting out. You can use a phrase like this when you see the heat is rising: "Maybe we're getting too heated up here, let's take a break for the moment, I'm going to go to the living room [or every other place you both can disconnect for a moment from the situation in your house] and we'll talk about it later with a clear mind". When the tension is lower and the environment more relaxed it will be easier to talk about anything, but do not let the topic cool down too much.

A last thought about this: deal with the present problems in the present, sharing with teenagers the vision you have on things as much closer to reality as possible. When you're stuck at home (or in other moments with lots of restrictions on physical social interaction with friends) many problems may seem bigger than what they are. For this reason you may try to deal with them as seriously as always, but in a more relaxed way (check Point 10 about this).

c) Listen to the elderly!

Many people think that the elderly is a category, a more vulnerable one on different levels, not only the medical one. The fear of contamination may help us to find ways to pay more attention to them, but at the same time it is exactly the contrary of what we have to think about when we actually talk to them.

We are aware of the indications of our healthcare authorities and of the protocols we have to follow to protect them, but then, when we're actually talking to them we should try not to overwhelm them with an excessive preoccupation.

Seniority is the moment of life that our society have less consideration of because the attention is focused almost always on young. Instead, getting old is just being the same person as always, just with a body that needs a little more maintenance. You are the same person! Besides, a person that has lived life without making all the mistakes we saw in point 1, 2 and 3, may feel as young and powerful as an adult or a teeneger. Sometimes even better.

Remember that physical and mental age are not always necessarily overlapping in any growth phase (that can be bad, but also good) and that some psychological changes produced by normal ageing may help people to be more healthy and take better care of themselves than when they were younger. It is not impossible to think that, apart from a different metabolism and a few aches and pains that we can keep at bay with medical check ups, some elderly people can feel subjectively in a very similar frame of mind as a younger person.

Now, knowing this, try to think of someone treating you as a baby when you're a young adult or a full grown adult. How would that make you feel? That's right, and that's exactly how an elderly person feels.

At the same time an elderly person may feel more alone in these times, especially if they are physically active but now they find themselves stuck at home because of the restrictions and quarantines laws or just to feel safer.

Try to encourage them to not increase their

isolation if not needed. Make a schedule of periodic family and friend contacts to improve their mood and to help them keep themselves socially active.

Remember then, that after quarantines and isolations they will be used to a frequent interaction, so remember to increase your presence progressively and do the same thing downwards (if it has to happen). This way you can avoid oppressing them with too much communication (it can happen too).

At the same time, but on the other side, if they suddenly feel an intensification of the communication from you, especially if associated with worries, it may be even worse for them to hear from you, so check the quality and not only the quantity of your communication with them too. Besides, if after these times of quarantine and restrictions they won't receive the same attention in quality or quantity they will suffer much more. So keep that in mind.

For this reason, try to plan now some future reunions with them even if you're not sure when it will happen. Talk about what you're going to do, plan it with them in detail, think about who's gonna be there, what your feelings will be. Try to think about everything you can discuss together in order to decrease the distance at least psychologically by thinking positively of the future.

Last but not least, even the Official Italian Psychologists Association says that we can help the elderly by joining one of our neighbours' initiatives.

There are active groups of neighbours and associations around you. Remember (to yourself and to your family) to use every precaution and sanitary protocols that your Health authorities give you to protect the elderly from the infection and be aware and up to date with certificates, permits, visiting hours or other restrictions your country is adopting at the time. Then, just enjoy your time together.

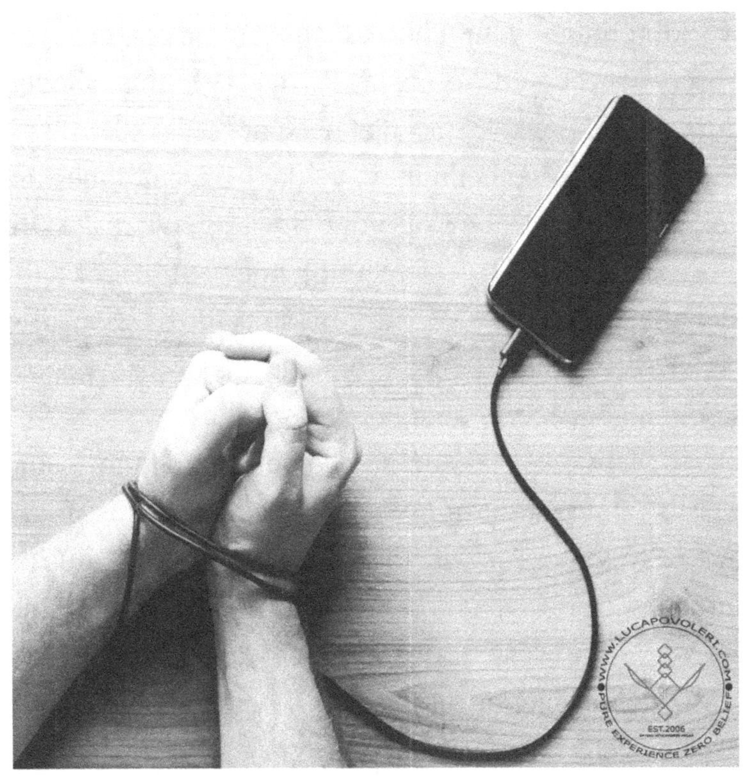

6) Find you best "Social" diet

Observe yourself while you're engaged in social networking. What do you like? A trick is to take a look at the first 10 posts on the home/wall and what kind of Advertising (ADS) is arriving to you based on last activities and preferences. Your interactions online are not only analized and piloted to influence you, they're somehow a reflection of what you "transmit" to the world through your choices and actions. Once you observed yourself for a while through this "Social mirror" just think: "Am I that person?"

Google something you liked a long time ago and enjoy the change on your Social networks ADS. You can even try something new, to look for something you always had a passion for or wished to do and never did, or check some details of that tv show so old no one talks about it anymore etc...

Networks can unite people sharing the same passion and in a lot of occasions it can be a way to get in touch with your friends. Nowadays though, during this pandemic and after that, they may represent an activity so present in our day that can be assimilated with binge eating or those famous high-calories snacks we take between meals.

Remember to rest your eyes every now and then, avoiding to spend a lot of uninterrupted time on your phone. If you're on a chat for some time already try to visualize yourself while pronouncing the words you're writing. You can also imagine yourself expressing in real life those emojis you like so much.

Also, if before the pandemic you were already spending a lot of time on your phone, now that it has become a necessary window to a real world that is temporarily out of reach, think about what you can do with it when you'll be once again out of the house or traveling.

It isn't impossible to find out now that you're a potential trekker just when the countryside and mountains are suddenly far from you. An idea you may keep in mind for when the house doors will be opened again.

7) Smart-Working as an occasion to optimize

Try to be your own boss and, if you're not already, learn how to be it!

Bosses are a symbolic hierarchical reference reflecting the need of a chain of command you have to respect. At the same time all the roles on an organization chart in any business have a space where you can find a certain degree of personal independence that gives you the chance of being a pure "follower" or "a boss of yourself".

Freelance professionals are the perfect example of these dynamics, but if you work in a company or for a small business you can always find the space to manage yourself and sometimes this can make the difference for professional growth. At the same time, taking full advantage of this even if only partial independence in your work to be proactive, may significantly increase your motivation and your pleasure while performing your working functions.

While smart-working, train yourself to be your boss. Be harsh and inflexible, but remember that your "worker" can be a "champion" of your company if you treat him/her well. Follow your normal rhythms and give yourself some time to take a breath. You're in your territory and you can find a positive distraction with literally everything you have around; this means you can slow down from time to time shifting even just for a few seconds the object of your attention. If the instant-break leads you to something natural or maybe outside a window it will be a very quick disconnection without losing focus. This means that then you can go back to work like you just refreshed your mind. At these times research shows that people tend to overwork while smart-working so you may need it.

Associating this disconnection with a voluntary change of your breathing rhythm and of your gaze direction can represent an instantaneous rest so powerful you can't even imagine. Instant-breaks like these can help you on many occasions when your work asks for prolonged attention to a subject for a long time. Everything you read here can be trained while smart-working but will be life-saver at the office or whatever it is your habitual working environment in the new normality.

Remember that, as said before, in your workplace someone may think you're working less at home, but it's usually not the case. On the contrary, if you don't check your schedule for work time and breaks you'll find an even more stressful situation at home instead than in your habitual workplace.

Find a quiet corner in your house where you can work in peace and if you don't have a dedicated space and you can't make you a stable one, try creating a perimeter around your working zone with objects that reminds you of your work and of your workplace. I know it's hard, but try to dress up like when you have to go out. If you usually wear a uniform and it's not the case to use it at home (*"Cum Grano Salis"* remember), find some different clothes than the ones you use in your "quality time" (the time dedicated to yourself, to relax and have fun, but with a special attention to the quality of the activity).

Do not change completely your working habits, don't take too many breaks but at the same time don't avoid taking breaks thinking you don't deserve them because when you'll be back to normal you'll have a harder time ajusting. So when you're on your break, enjoy it to the full, you're in a pandemic situation after all, and after that, you may be deserve it. Of course if you're not working well that's a different story, maybe you can take time to find something else or to find a better motivation.

The Italian Official Italian Psychologists Association suggests that during this time you can take advantage of the situation to eat healthier. You can even think about how to bring this new good habit into your working environment when it is compatible.

Try to become and be aware of the difference between real life and quarantine/restrictions life, but try to adapt to both because one can improve the other. Sometimes we have already thought of the best solution to improve our working life and we just need time to think about it. Now we have that time...

Last but not least, take your time to study the lighting in your work area and if you find the perfect arrangement make it your habitual working place while home and study a way to have the same light on your your workplace. The light has to be strong enough to avoid straining your eyes, especially if you work with your laptop for a long periods of time each day. If it is possible, try to use both natural and artificial light: this way you can save on your energy bills, help the planet and help yourself by taking care of both your visual and emotional health.

8) *Move that body, move those emotions!*

Think that your body is like your city at this time. There is no one in the street (or it should be this way during lockdowns) and after quarantine periods there will be more people around but with rules and restrictions.

Now think that your heart, your liver, your intestine and above all your brain are like this city where there's no people or less people that are working (that also reflects the lower activity needs of our society, but no everytime of our life too... we are still living). This is the only occasion when online videos, free "live" workshops and Apps can really help you out (Check Point 15 because not all that glitters is gold).

Connect with other people having the same philosophy to be active like you. Remember that if you aim at a situation of low effort maximum results it's ok, you don't have to build a prison body out of boredom... but don't get too lazy now, going back to activity will be much more difficult later on.

On the contrary, try to keep more or less the same pace you were having before the pandemic and follow your natural inclinations for sport so that when a new normality will arrive, you won't lose your extra efforts. Unless you find a new passion that can survive in the new normality of course.

Participate in online lessons, get into groups and find the energy and motivation with people of the same mindset and goals as your own.

Always remember to check your health status before beginning any aerobic or anaerobic training or class,especially new ones. If you have physical or metabolic problems always ask a doctor first. Try to follow only personal trainers with medical official degrees, physiotherapist etc... or any formation category recognized by your country as "official". It's not a good moment to risk it, even if the people you want to follow seem to be good.

Besides, not everything that seems good on paper is good for "you". Overdoing it at a moment when the health system is overrun because of Covid is not a good idea. They may not have enough people to check on you if you hurt yourself so it is as shortsighted as inactivity. "*Cum Grano Salis*", works for this aspect of life too. I will never underline enough to my Life Adventurers: remember to take life with a pinch of salt, do not over do it.

Generally speaking, try to dedicate 30 minutes every day to move your body to keep your metabolism active and improve your mood with natural endorphins.

During lockdown and, of course, every day of your life, especially during long days working at a desk, always remember to get up every 45-50 minutes and, if you work on a screen, rest your eyes for 10-15 minutes every hour. When you work from home you can do that easily and when you're back at the workplace you can use those moments to deal with off-screen work activities so you're still being productive while maintaning your health. Of course, resting your eyes while scrolling your phone doesn't count...

9) *Retake contact with people who are good for you*

One of the main causes of stress during lockdowns and in the following phases of new normalities is isolation. Sometimes it is imposed by the authorities, sometimes by fear and excessive prudence even when it is not necessary. Thanks to technology we can stay in touch with family, friends, even with our partner on some occasions (check Point 10). There are a lot of different Apps that can reduce that distance and reunite us with groups and friends that we used to meet and spend time with: for breakfast, happy hours, birthdays... even if we're physically far away.

At the same time we're used to living an accelerated lifestyle and that sometimes adds distance between some of the people you once knew and that were good for you. When we talk of personal wellbeing during Covid (and after that hopefully) we shouldn't really talk only of "surviving", but also of improving our life taking the advantage of that extra time (check Point 14).

How many times have you thought of that friend that you lost on the way to your present life... Maybe with time we already reconnected with her/him on some social network, but on that occasion you may just have had a few words, a few "likes" and nothing more. Even the virtual territory of apparent hyper-connection has its rules and, if you don't pay the fee as it is requested, you risk to lose sight of this friend again in the strong waves of algorithms.

So why don't you use this occasion to say hi and ask how life is for them during quarantine (or later in the new normalities)? Maybe some (self)irony (check

Point 1) can help to break the ice, especially if we're in contact with people so constantly alarmed, afraid and pessimist (as it happens) that makes all the situation much harder than it already is.

In this case using the lockdowns, the following restrictions or the new normalities as an excuse to get closer together, a perfect opportunity to positivize the situation creating a shared experience which is one of the most important foundations of human relations.

Beyond that, sometimes remembering good memories spent together is an ideal way to reconnect to a part of ourselves that we may have lost and with those lost parts we may find an occasion to re-discover resources or skills we have forgotten about. Or maybe it's just the perfect way to make a virtual trip down memory lane in other times and places that may lead to future reunions and shared plans in the #postcovid19 life.

10) *Rediscover your partner and find yourself again in the process*

If you have a partner, at home or far away because of the Covid, this distance / uninterrupted presence may be an opportunity to get deeper involved in your relationship and to stabilize all the positive effects you may have co-created with her/him in this nonstandard situation. It seems quite difficult to understand when you can't see each other and you miss each other emotionally, physically, spiritually or instead when you have to forcefully see each other for a long time, in a communal space that inevitably seems to be getting a little smaller day by day.

Both kind of situations are very stressful for people during lockdown and even in life after this before the #postcovid19 world. In fact we'll see that sometimes distance and presence may be subjective.

First, you have to keep in mind that this situation is extreme, out of the ordinary and it will take a good deal of patience, maybe more than normal. To Life Adventurers though this can represent a chance to go back to the origins, create a second honeymoon or even to re-discover that person with totally new features different from the one you used to know after many years of relationship.

Unlike other points, this one needs special attention to the definition of the word "couple" or "partner". That's because the definition may have so many shades of grey (definitely more than 50) that makes it difficult to enclose them all in a few lines. A solution to this "impasse" is to consider that every kind of relationship that two people may feel comfortable to define as "couple" has the right to be part of this Point.

We're talking about both emotional and physical

relational bonds so why would we settle for less? There is no need for a manual that says you're a couple or not, everything depends on your personal definition, when shared with the other(s) included.

Constant presence may be stressful for anyone, so in these times it's a perfect excuse to train yourself to subjectively perceive and create distance without losing good emotions in the process. It's the time to suggest moments of solitude and isolation to your partner, which is a healthy habit in normal life and would be even more useful in #postcovid19 life. If you have the space at home to spend part of the day alone in separate places it can be an interesting game. So close the doors, you do your activity alone, although a quick kiss in the corridor is admitted... Do not be afraid of creating distance, it can be a friendly ally for everyone if we get to know her better.

When you want to spend time together then (please note the word "want"), try to increase your action power in the restricted situation you're in by sharing the creative part of the plan you're making. Sharing in an action too. After you find distance, now any activity that you usually do by yourselves alone you can do it trying to remember when you were dating. Share the objectives of the day and rethink the way you share the chores that (hopefully) you already shared before.

Do not forget that this has to be playful. Get creative, go back to the dimension of playing, to see the game inside what's happening to you; it's really important in relationships to keep it easy although it is not an excuse to take feeling for granted.

People in relationships are and always will be separate universes that twirl together because of feelings, plans of life, attraction... The secret sometimes is to think of yourself as individual people that choose each other every day for the reasons that brought you initially together (and new ones too). Being able to have fun is very important when you're with somebody. Even playing (together) may help you during these hard times, mixing it up, changing rules and the roles.

On the other hand, when you and your partner are apart, technology offers creative solutions to feel together. Temporary loss of physical intimacy may be considered this way: temporary. Think of this time as a historical moment that will end soon, it's not a never ending journey. With the right dose of creativity even distance can be under control. Instead of seeing it so negatively try to think about it like a chance to share moments that weren't shared before. It can be a step forward in a relationship at an early phase or it can represent instead that pause that maybe you never asked for or maybe you never needed, but which is healthy from time to time. The only limit to a relationship is the feeling and the resilience, the ability to adapt and find creative solutions with right amount self-limitation and exploration of yourself and the other, always being respectful of each other.

Maybe it's not necessary to play "fake dates", we're not in a movie, but don't forget to check your look when you're celebrating a special occasion, exactly as you were doing when you were going out. Plan a romantic dinner, movie night, series binge watching as if it were a date night. Dress up, take an extra shower even you already took one in the morning like when you were preparing for a special night, light a candle, put on some music... you have your secret moves, use them. Original is nice.

It is important to find a couple occasions for these little date nights in your week to find a way of "going out", evoke the feeling, even if you can't really go out or if you can do it but with restrictions like a curfew, masks, limitations etc.... it may seem weird, maybe even forced and unnatural sometimes and it's obviously just a temporary fix (Super-living humans won't make this pandemic a "forever" situation, this book is about this too), but remember, those small details may make all the difference.

In case of a conflict in a couple: if you see some tension between you, try to deal with it before getting to explicit anger. Try to avoid being too sensitive to mood changes in your partner though, they may be exasperated by the pandemic isolation effects. Respect the need for silence from the other person if you feel tension, but avoid building an unbreakable wall out of it. Remember that you're living a situation which is not normal or familiar and that your emotions can be consequently more intense than usual.

A trick: if you get to the moment when you're actually feeling angry with your partner and a fight begins, follow your feelings and try to release some steam for both of you, avoid hurting yourselves too much and try the game of "I'm wrong... - Me too".

What is this relational game about? First, when you can use it: it may work either in the moment when everything just went well and you need time to process or if you're taking a break (as I suggest in Point 5 with teenagers, it works perfectly with everyone at any age) to cool down a little before going back to solve the problem together.

The point is to acknowledge a part of your responsibility in the co-production of the cause of your fight. First goes one of you, than the other. But... and this is essential, during this moment of taking responsibility (which is hard), the other can't say a world. Not even to appreciate it (and absolutely not if you don't). Then, if it feels natural, just hug. Or not. Follow your instinct.

Very often people tend to think they're "right" when having a fight. We're victims of a competitive society that divides you into winners and losers. This is even harder to be self-aware of, if your quarrel is heavily affected by hard-to-recognise exterior causes like the pandemic pyschlogical and social construct. Usually it's a communication problem that may have been present before and you're able to see it only now. Real power for super-living humans here is to accept and learn to see our responsibility even when we think we haven't done anything bad. That will set us free from the idea of "blame" and "guilt" by considering every problem as co-created. You and your partner are together even in this and if you can solve it together you will grow together.

Truly emotional mature couples are the ones that see beyond black and white, right and wrong, guilty and victim. They're the ones that live better in their relationship, regardless of the time they have been or will be together.

That being said this doesn't mean that

sometimes people fight with a partner for many reasons and that things can be much more complex than what can be said in a psychological first aid 101 manual like this one. That's the moment you should seek professional help specific for you and/or your relationship.

Last point: in case of complete failure of your relationship, when you get to the point that you can see only a break up, a separation or even a divorce. If you reach this conclusion during lockdowns and times with many restrictions to freedom, do still follow your decision of course. Resisting against a flow so strong as a breaking up relationship when you see no hope and do it in a limited psycho-physical space like during these days is at least as negative as leaving it dissolved into nothing.

Although if you do find yourselves in this situation, do not exaggerate your reactions, try to close it peacefully and leave at least a small corner in your heart for a chance to look at it again at the end of lockdown. In these moments everything related to feelings will be exalted by the stress caused by the pandemic.

Of course in a very small portion of statistical cases we can find situations objectively inhumane or unacceptable. Remember: even if the world has slowed down, justice and professional help is there for you.

May your relationship, wether it is working or your're breaking up, always be considered as such only when it is based on an irrevocable respect between human beings. Zero exceptions.

Whatever stress you're feeling or self-limitations you're living in, there's no relationship whatsoever if you don't respect the primary human rights for every part involved in the relationship.

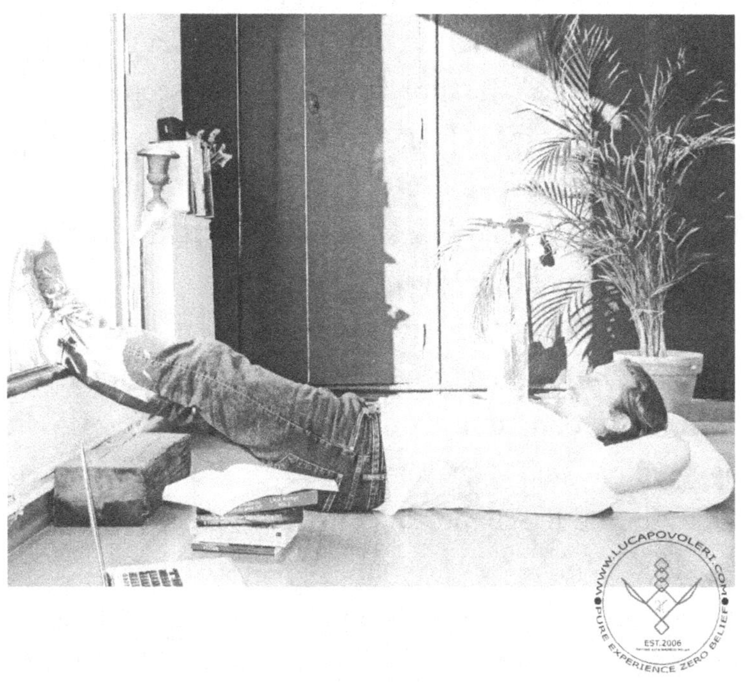

11) Remember to rest

When we're in a lockdown we may have the feeling of being on vacation. In fact being most of the tested positive asyntomatic and mostly forced to stay home on medical leave, sometimes we feel we don't understand exactly if we're sick or just "paused" by the situation. So after lockdown the work flow will be slower, maybe we lost our work and we have to find a new one, maybe weare waiting to go back to our work when all the defined "non-essential" activities will be activated again... so in all the above and similar "suspended life" situations our days may seem endless. This is true for most people suffering from "absence of activity" and for those who, on the contrary, are working around the clock to save our lives. We'll be talking about both of them.

For those who are quarantined this means that when bedtime arrives you don't feel tired, you may be able to sleep but your dream phases will be hyperactive and you may wake up earlier or more times during the night. The effects of every form taken by sleep deprivation are hard to self-evaluate and can be disastrous on health. Sleeping well is the key for a lighter mood too, which is, together with good diet and balanced physical activity (I know, it would be easier if one thing were the solution to everything, but we're a complex interaction of cross feedbacks through all our systems) are essentials for a strong and healthy immunitary system.

Thanks to a good nights sleep and all the above interactions you may result positive to Covid and still, if you don't have other risk factors like cardiac, immunitary or pulmonary conditions or other disease you have a good chance to pass the infection as asymptomatic or mildly symptomatic. This means that even if you catch the virus (any virus by the way, not just Covid) you'll have more "weapons" to fight your inner virological war and a good chance to win it over without that much of an effort.

Numbers can be scary but this is the reality of the majority of people infected with Covid. The virus (at least in the original form) seems to have actually a low mortality rate so quarantine and following restrictions are strategies adopted to lower the high rates of contagiousness which is it's worst feature. Besides, this helps the hospitalary system by avoiding it to be overloaded by patients which is important not only for medical resources but also to keep health workers more rested and more effective helping those who have from moderate to severe symptoms. Remember that there are thousands of other illnesses that don't stop existing for Covid too...

This is why an aware citizen self-limitation is needed: to protect other people, but yourself too under the form of easier health system access if you need it.

Sometimes your health may seem so good and unaffected by anything that you may underestimate the positive effects of a good sleeping habit and of a regular disconnection from stress on the medium and long run (Check point 15). It is important to always be attentive to this when you're in a lockdown or after that (hopefully soon), so try to consider them well while thinking of your health and wellbeing.

It may be a good idea to invest at least an hour a day away from social networks and news channels just to read a book, drink some herbal tea, listen to relaxing music. That would help to create a good sleep condition when you're going to bed later. This is what the Official Italian Psychologists Association suggests.

Beyond that, try not to change your circadian rhythm (the sleep-wake patterns in your day) too much. For instance if you usually wake up early in the morning for work, try to do the same. If you're in quarantine and you usually wake up before dawn for commuting to work and you don't need to that, you don't have to wake up two hours before of course, but you can still wake up early to keep your body used to it... clearly common sense "docet" (literally: "your common sense teaches you").

Keeping a "similar" day rhythm as you had/have while fully operational is a good help even for those mysterious and uncomfortable headaches that seem to appear with no apparent reason or known etiology. Even a migraine can be fought sometimes by maintaining similar circadians rhythms on working days and free days.

Our body has a rhythm. It's exactly like a heartbeat but it's more complex and it goes through every organic functions that keeps us alive. Of course an exaggeratedly strict habit isn't the answer here and it won't be ever. In fact that would be even unhealthy sometimes, especially in quarantine, lockdowns and new normalities... That being said, having a schedule to follow in your daytime, especially in these historiacal time, is one of the best and easiest ways to counteract the secondary effects of restrictions and isolation.

Let's talk about sanitary workers, the true heroes of the battle as the media say, and, with them, everyone working to keep our life in the city active. Those who provide lights, clean streets, food, order and the quickest reply to emergencies etc... well for you a good sleep is even more important but in a slightly different way.

Without a good sleep, the doctor, the nurse and all the health workers can't really count on the necessary cognitive and emotional health they need to make good decisions. They will lack the strength for winning the huge battle they fight every day against the virus and to protect themselves from infection too. Remember that for people in this work category a good sleep is a responsibility as well as a right.

Besides, to those who work for health and for the city services: remember that your job is a team effort and that the weight of the psychological experience that you're bearing these days has to be shared with your team. Be a good team player, help each other and be aware that this is trench warfare until the science finds a way to neutralize the virus. After that you may consider evaluating the damage left on you after long months of stress.

The mentalization of this experience may bring to someone like you and especially to some of those who faced the first waves of deaths, similar symptoms (but not necessarily the same, we don't have to always "psycopathologize" everything) of the PTSD.

That frustration and impotence especially at the beginning of the pandemic and during the fortunately almost all better-contained following waves of contagion will take a toll on people's psychology and it will be worse for those living with it at close quarters more than others.

Luckily, you're not in a trench now and there are lots of ways to relax while self-healing part of the damage (self)inflicted to your mind. And, luckily for you, many of them are free or almost free and online too.

Try to give yourself a few minutes before going to sleep just to elaborate and process your daily events.

Even if you get home tired, do not go from 100% to 0% in a second, take a small break, a parenthesis in your life narration, just to breathe and meditate. This has to be an add up to all other recovery activities with networks, TV, movie, gym etc... it is a different moment, one for yourself and with yourself only.

If you have "no time", that's maybe an excuse, you only need 90-120 seconds on a day. Maybe you even can try it before or during a break at work, if you have a little time to rest.

Take 3 deep breaths, then breathe normally for 20 seconds, take 2 deep breaths, then breath normally for 20 seconds, then take 1 last deep breath and breathe normally. Just this... A trick might be to focus your attention on the sole of the feet or in the feeling produced by their contact with the floor. Alternatively, if you're laying down, focus on the weight of your heels, pelvis or shoulders on the surface on which you're laying down.

During these 90-120 seconds of "you-time",, listen to what's happening around you as a silent observer that chooses the no-reaction approuch to external stimuli and try to be aware only of your respiration.

This exercise is really easy, you don't have to believe to an eastern or ancient culture theory to practice it, so it's very useful for everyone and helps with stress, fear, anxiety and mood swings. During and after the pandemic of course.

12) Invest in new skills

Your skills are life toolboxes. They are the foundation of your passions, your work skills and sometimes of your talents too. But how we got what whe have and how we improve them. Some of them have a genetic basis and predisposition, but they be inactive if you don't know yourself and choose them actively. And self-awareness is the first-step.

If you have more time now it will be inevitable to reach that moment where you'll think about all the choices you made in your life. Sometimes we tend to think too much on our mistakes (sometimes not enough though), but any choice we make is simply a new step toward a different path. Life Adventures can take us in different directions and thinking of the mistakes we made has to be a healthy way to learn and not a reason to be obsessed about something. It would be the same as feeling guilty for falling down a couple of years ago on a trekking excursion. First of all if you're still alive then it wasn't so dramatic after all. In fact that rock, exactly to the contrary of what you're thinking may have just been a warning not to talk too much while walking, or to better watch our step and take time to think prudently when choosing the right shoes or boots for the path we're taking.

People with no complaints at all instead may have to be more aware of those around them because they may be affected by the "chosen one" paradigm. There's a very microscopic chance that you reached enlightenment and those who have reached it might be aware of the loss it means to live and choose. If you think you have made everything fine until now maybe you should widen your idea of humanity and reduce the idea you have of yourself. Just a little, just to check better. It may be a shield you raised around your heart for a low self esteem induced by your environment. Your path is easier though: just keep doing what you're doing, just check your steps from time to time if you're 100% of the time because maybe you're overestimating it.

Luckily most of you aren't going to be obsessed or overconfident of your past choices and you'll just be in the perfect position to look back to those activities you would have loved to have done in the past and to other activites that you perhaps sacrificed during your choice-making to make space for those you actually undertook. Luckily many of those activities are still in your reach. Maybe they won't be the origin of a new path, but they may help to optimize the time we don't know what to do with and they may be a good way to find a new treasure in ourselves.

Let's take back our passion for art, that english course we wanted to take to improve our international connections, those DIY videos or that self help book we left gathering dust on the bedside table for months. As you have a limited time to spend on it (quarantine and lockdowns will end...) we can have the psychological upper hand to kick our laziness ("I may take some effort for a few days and I can leave it whenever I want after all"), our perfectionism fetish

("I'm taking advantage of the time to do something that will improve my skills") or our self-sabotages ("No one will chastise me here in this quiet corner of my house, I will be with myself and with my passion...) whatever happens, happens"). In this case not being too "Social" about it helps much more than you may think.

When you think of yourself, you have a distinctive image in your mind "I am good at..." and any person in the world can list at least three things that she/he is feeling able to do. At the same time though, there are many "soft skills", lateral skills, hidden in what we socially call useless skills. Some of those are invisible to us for this reason, social approval, and that's why we consider them less important or essential to us, because we tend to reduce everything to "basic usefulness for a human". Those "soft skills" instead can contribute a lot to improve even our baseline human functions and our overall usefulness, but only if we look at them from an advanced perspective.

A businessman knowing his/her wines, a journalist with green thumb, a doctor who can sing... all these soft skills that we train in on our spare time, can give at least a small "bonus" to our main skills: a better chance to convince new clients to choose us, create harmony in different parts of an article, keep emotions at bay while dealing with patients. That's just a few examples, but the skys the limit.

So this is a way you can use that extra time created by this pandemic. You can make yourself more valuable and add some new positive experiences to your life. It can even be an occasion to change your world in an indirect way, acting effectively on those dynamics that you always failed to change while trying to deal directly with them.

This is one of the hardcore differences between surviving and super-living life: everything, even what society collectively think is less important in life, can be to the contrary an instrument, a special feature that helps you pass from auto-pilot to being "you".

13) Humans do not live of coronavirus alone

It is natural, while dealing with quarantine and new normalities, to live having every moment in front of you with the cause of this global intervention. This time it is Covid but similar situations have happened before with terrorism. This new form of collective fear will change the perception of things until we have the most efficient measures to deal with the sanitary emergency around the globe. Not an ideal situation of course and maybe this fear will try to stay with us even after things have improved.... which will force us to take even more seriously every tool that transforms that "fear" into prevention and caution created by awareness.

The world united back in the day thanks to the internet, the markets, mass tourism and that means that even our lives are intertwined. This is a truth that was clear before, but today it's clearer than ever. We can't forget that there have been plagues since the begining of time, so it was only a question of time before this happened once again, even in today's modern society. Luckily there are many ways to live with and avoid Covid.

Follow the instructions of the health authority, stay at home if thats what is asked of you, limit contact with people, use masks, keep social distancing etc, etc... it's quite simple and it's valid, whether you're in a quarantine situation or in the new normalities, whether you're working or you're studying presentially. Delegating at least part of the worry on something we don't have a direct control over is the best way to keep the right distance from it. We're a society, that means, in a way at least, we can count on some protection coming from that.

Do not live in fear, we have many weapons in this battle... maybe the virus took us all off guard at the beginning, but we're reacting. Anyhow, even if we were facing a lethal overwhelming situation, it is much better to fight till the end with a heart filled with a complete spectrum of emotions, each one of them taken with the right weight, and not just with fear.

An exercise you can do is to think about the way your life will change after this and to what has already changed. It is not important if we think it is transitory or definitive (although very few things in life are definitive...). What is going to have a long term influence over us will be all the changes made Covid Construct. It's true that after all of this needed immobilization, work life will recover part of it's pre-pandemic strength, but still it is a good moment to have a little heart-to-heart conversation with ourselves to widen our global awareness.

Here we are a blue planet in the middle of an immense universe and, as many poets, philosophist and singers have told to us over centuries, we can try to resize the importance we give our existence, we can try being more peaceful and tolerant, being able to forgive our own mistakes and the mistakes of others. This doesn't mean we have to reach such extremes like loving universally everything and everyone, we sort of need to keep a certain "meritocracy" in life and that's what we're looking for, that's is Super-living Life Adventurers path.

The only way to achieve this is our ability for self-evaluation: it is very likely that we're not Zeros or One-Hundreds, but together we can try to obtain a baseline in our common rights as worker for instance, something that we didn't achieve before because everyone was voicing their own opinions without finding common grounds.

The most important thing now is to get in contact with your deeper meaning. Who are you really? Why do you exist? Try to separate the blind instinct of living from your choice to live. This will give you a different value of yourself and to the events you're living now and #postcovid19.

Remember that emergencies existed before the pandemic, maybe if you recall them, you can take away the "absolute protagonism" of the "doomsday villain" of the moment.

Then, once you've made peace with this (but you have to do it right, it won't do you any good to negate events), go back to your tv series, talk about something else and make new projects realistic with the pandemic and the new normalities so they can live on and prosper even after this ends. Do not let the

Covid and the Psychological and Social Construct of Covid control your mind. Think the right amount of thoughts about taking care of yourself, and then, keep on living.

14) "Positivize" your story

What's negative about your personal story? If you checked last chapters you may become familiar with the idea of "positivizing" things. In my line of work I use this specific term to change polarity on a human dimension or a topic. Does that mean it will be "good" after that? That's not the answer. Positive and negative are relative concepts and at the end of "Super-living" it will be clear. For now let's focus on your story alone and let implicits do their work.

It can be interesting to think about what's happening to you and change your perspective flipping things around for a moment. Positive Thinking is a recent part of psychology that has created big changes on people's subjective wellbeing. We can see it on TV, on social media, in a cinema movie, narration topics and even on influencers activities.

Sometimes though this attitude gets out of hand and creates a tendency to see things in a definitely excessive positive way. That made people go so far from reality in later times that give birth, as a reactive opposite response, to a wave of dangerous senseless alarmism and excessive sensitivity to almost every aspect of reality. It was a dynamic pre-existing coronavirus and this may be a good time to change it.

Let's try to see things in a positive way without seeing everything through rose-coloured glasses because we'll be so used to it that we may be oversensitive to a no-pink situation (even if it's just purple...). An example, a funny but realistic one, are the memes created on the odd "toilet paper emergency" (that never existed but it was created or empowered by senseless alarmism). These memes helped to make fun out of it but still fed the idea of the fake emergency during the first weeks of the pandemic.

There's no need to repeat the "everything's gonna be fine" mantra. Try to have a more realistic view of the specific situation. We already saw in the last chapters what we can do to help others (and ourselves too in the process) so now let's try to focus on how to narrate our best personal story as an individual by un-pinking the situation or de-alarmating it.

The Pandemic here is merely a pretext to do just that, but this was valid before, and it will be useful through any phase of the new normalities and beyond that, in the new #postcovid19 world. Right now we can apply it to those behaviours we can assume to cope with isolation or with being close to people in small spaces for instance... be creative in it's application, everything falls in this strategy's area of effect once you control it. You have the chance to change something by changing the way you narrate it to yourself.

For example: you forgot the milk and you don't have any milk left at home during a lockdown. Going out to buy groceries is clearly permitted, but if you go out once it's ok, going out twice only for milk may increase risk of infection for you or other people. Do you want to do that for milk? Do you need it? Well you can still do it, but instead of going out again or feeling "wrong" for your mistake, why can't you simply find other recipes or other options for a milk-less breakfast? Changing an habit can be a good psychological reinforcement to remember milk next time and at the same time to enjoy the moment and what you already have. That is achieved by changing a word in your life narration: you may "need" milk or "want" milk.

Another example with a different twist which is more usual after lockdowns: you're on a train while commuting to work. You're in the middle of hundreds of masks, maybe it's hot in there and, even with social distance applied, you may feel everyone too close to you... Instead of focusing on your emotions, why don't you ask yourself what's the meaning to the expression of that faraway-nearby person car while holding on to the straps or sitting down between other people? What is (s)he narrating?
Remember that we give so much importance to words and images, but just a few of us can read body language, so don't judge yourself on performance during this exercise, just try it and flow with it. Pure Experience, Zero Belief...

This change of narration works on perspective. Besides helping you to keep your emotions in check while living a averegely low pandemic-related stressful situation like being in a train with many people, this will be useful to be more empathetic to others now, and in the future, when masks won't cover our smiles anymore.

Try to see your own personal story as the one of a main character of course, but merged and mixed together with the personal narrations of your family, your loved ones, your friends and try to put yourself in their shoes. Imagine yourself being them in their life's story like you and see it through your own eyes.

Remember that if we are connected through networks and, in a way, even through this shared experience of the Covid, our existence as species may have a real collective dimension. That means you're not alone and that even small changes in you may have a repercussion on the others.

Once you understand this dynamic you can begin to try narrating your own experiences, in the present and in the future, in different ways.

Do not lose your sense of reality of course though, we're not making comics or a movie here, this is your life we're talking about.

Instead of trying to change your all story, try to focus only on small details, being aware that every in every event of life resides an occasion to positively transform yourself and our collective narration through a change of perspective.

15) Select your sources of information

As this Point is completely dedicated to selecting your information which can free your mind from interference of misinformation to avoid the excess of fear and frustration while reducing the vulnerability to fake news, I'll be brief...

On health topics look for information only on official channels of health authorities. No influencers, news, no friends doctors, online video etc... full stop.

If you want to look at alternative sources try to keep what you find to yourself. Being unsure about the quality of the content, if you're wrong you'll make much more damage than helping people by sharing whatever you may feel is right. Many fake news involve an implicit or explicit request for sharing by creating psychological pressure that works on generosity, helpfulness, drama... you can feel it, the uncomfortable push to action, so do not lose your anti-conformism right now, do the opposite!

Find a balance between being up to date to all news in real time and avoiding official information at all.

Keep in mind that society list "information" among the services to citizens considered "essentials" . The same information that in any form we know needs sparkling and high pitched emotions to keep the attention of an audience every day more vulnerable to boredom. That's a fact and common knowledge already.

This means that there is a lot of emphasis while making the news, especially on those emotions that we know that drive people to stay in front of the media and listen. For this reason, even if we're aware of these dynamics, their unconscious impact on us is still quite strong, so if we can't limit the time we dedicate to information in any way, we may be influenced by the emotions they're impregnated with. Even if we feel we're strong willed.

Besides, try to select sources (even official ones) that don't leave you with a "fear" sensation. Even if fear is right sometimes, a good "different ally", and even if it is the normal reaction associated with some aspects of the news, this feeling, when abused, lowers our morale and our immune system, creating stress and a feeling of helplessness.

This dynamic has a good side though: people creating that feeling in your life are the ones that are more likely to be recognized as "toxic people" in common language (remember this is not the case people who share their feelings and accept yours too like suggested in Point 1 and 5) and you can use this information to protect yourself. These people will be hyperactive these times, whether they are creating excessive fear of rage, they will be feasting on it.

Another very important topic in these times is using networks, social media, influencers, videos etc... just as an "inspiration", not as solid "information". Take your distance especially from someone who is completely sure of everything (s)he says which is not the behaviour of a real expert, especially while considering topics on which our science knowledge is still very limited.

Remember then that if there are specific protocols to produce medicines or to consider any form of research true and real, that's because if you want to be really sure of something you have to study it thoroughly. Very thoroughly! So, just live the "common sense" aside on this... let it be just one voice among others, an inspiration maybe, but don't let yourself be influenced by it.

Keep in mind that even if our "visual" society creates the opportunity for very talented (and resourceful) communication-people to create empires of followers, this doesn't really guarantee in any way the quality of contents. In fact, sometimes that huge public is just a guarantee for the contrary.

Try to find the essence of what you get from your information sources and try to hear different voices if you're not sure about something, always giving priority to official channels. Do not follow what "makes sense" to you if you're not an expert yourself (even as an expert you should have access to raw data too and study it very well before talking right?) and be wary of experts with no officially recognised formation on the specific topic they're talking about.

Remember that truth is far from being "free"

(exactly the opposite people sell you) and that to actually achieve it yourself you usually have to make sacrifices, study a lot and make extra efforts to separate it from general interference.

In conclusion, keep your mind open, select carefully what you bring inside of your life and when to believe in something.

Last but not least, try not to give too many importance to raw numbers everyday, it will be at the end of this world emergency that health experts reading real data will be able to give a valuable meaning to them.

16) Connect with your Neighbourhood

The human being exists as an individual, but, if we want to see it from a different perspective, putting the survival baseline function as the foundation for more evolved ones, our dimension as Human Species is, first of all, the very foundation of our existence. Species --> geographical territories --> relational groups --> then us, as individuals.

We don't have to go too far, literally and metaphorically, to see that our neighborhood is the closest human territory for us and it's a space, an area that we can have direct experience over. Furthermore, there are many neighborhood initiatives we can join during quarantine and after that.

There are neighborhood apps, communities on social media and even whatsapp groups you can connect to. They're involved in many solidarity initiatives for people that may need help too if you like to join them.

Actively participating in the development of your closer community is a great way to improve your morale, your self-efficacy (the subjective sensation to be able to produce results as a result of our efforts) and your usefulness.

Search online on the map your neighborhood local shops that can provide first necessity services. Remember that in some occasion a small grocery shop may have the same products you're going to buy in a supermarket. Choosing a good small business close to you is not only a way to support your local community, you're reducing the time you pass in the street, you reduce concentration in supermarkets and you can even find inspiration in local products that you can't find on a crowded standardized white shelf.

Besides, your neighborhood will be essential to recuperation when we'll be through this pandemic. Globalization has made us forget that usually what's closeer to us (the famous Kilometer Zero) is more economical than "low cost", maybe not always quantitatively, but for the services for which you're paying the price: you're paying more product and less taxes, transport etc...

Local producers are the ones that create the product and you're paying directly for their work, their usefulness, their art, their humanity. The same thing we hope happens to us every time we work...
Last but not least, keep in mind this: the more developed is your neighborhood, the more it will be able to resist in a crisis situation and the more attention it will get when the city authorities manages public resources.
As always, but it's true, together we're stronger.

Where can I find more help?

Sometimes the problems are bigger than us and we may need some professional help. We consider weakness being unable to solve everything via a Youtube tutorial, but sometimes delegate the solution is a good idea.

First of all remember to check the information you have (Check point 15) and give your trust only when you see it fit.

If you find a psychologist that inspires trust there are a lot of free psycholoy services active these days.

And if you need a professional "Empowerer" check www.lucapovoleri.com.

Pure Experience, Zero Belief.

BIO

Luca Povoleri De Las Heras is a trilingual cognitive-systemic psychologist. He's a fitness lover, cooking explorer and aware spirituality guide too working as an avertising photoshooting producer in Spain and always looking for the perfect combination of Communication and Ethics in success.

After years of experience he created "Optima Vita 360° - Life & business", a multi-disciplinary psychology-based coaching system based on his international experience in multinational companies and clients of his professional practice in Milan and Madrid.

Using the metaphore of Life Adventurers he teaches meditation through mindfulness, guided experiences and Featherless Shamanism. The objective is to optimize emotional/energetic balance in high performance situations and everyday life.

He loves to work to distinguish the wide and comprehensive, but still scientific, vision of health and wellness from the dazzling lights of the holistic world by creating empowerment events for rational people in Europe.

His motto "Pure Experience, Zero belief" is the filter he created to help people, especially rational ones that are usually excluded, by using the magic of unconscious symbolism which is the deeper foundation of motivation. Personal and Professional evolution for him has always to be integrated with the common evolution as human species.

Shenda Cregan is a British bilingual upcycling artist who lives in Barcelona Spain. She spends her time designing unique pieces for her company "La Shenda Deco". An avid art buff who enjoys rooting around the many flea markets around Barcelona to find unusual objects.

After 40 years in Spain and 20 years working in graphic design for various companies she decided to reinvent herself and started transforming old furniture and objects from drab to fab unique deco items.

In this throw away world in which we live in there is little regard for old furniture and bits and bobs of a bygone era, most of it is often deemed as mere useless trash, but sometimes old can be surprising, old can be trendy. Being a woman in what is perceived as more of a male profession there have been many comments over the years such as; " But do you really do all the woodwork/upholstery yourself? Doesn't your husband help with most of it" etc.

Growing up with a father who was a carpenter he taught the right way to measure, the importance and respect for one's tools and that anyone can dream to create, and create to dream…

Her motto is that change is always possible no matter how lost the item appears, even with woodworm we all have the capacity for renewal, so as the butterfly pops out of the chrysalis her art pieces evolve towards their new life.

It was a reflective journey and pleasure to help Luca with this manual.

www.ingramcontent.com/pod-product-compliance
Lightning Source LLC
Chambersburg PA
CBHW070812240726
48654CB00007B/317